577.7
GOW

Gowell, Elizabeth
  Tayntor.

Fountains of life.

C.1

$23.00

34880030010693

DATE			

FOUNTAINS OF LIFE
THE STORY OF DEEP-SEA VENTS

ELIZABETH TAYNTOR GOWELL

A FIRST BOOK

Franklin Watts
A Division of Grolier Publishing
New York • London • Hong Kong • Sydney
Danbury, Connecticut

For Matthew

The author would like to thank former *Alvin* pilot and deep-sea researcher Cindy Lee Van Dover, now an Associate Professor of Oceanography at the University of Alaska, Fairbanks, for her technical review of the manuscript.

Cover painting by Pedro J. Gonzalez

Illustrations by Joe LeMonnier

Photographs ©: Alice Alldredge: 39; Cindy Lee Van Dover: 15; Galaxy Contact/Explorer: 26; National Geographic Society: 16, 48 (Emory Kristoff); National Park Service, Yellowstone National Park: 34; NOAA: 33, 36; Peter Girguis: 42; Photo Researchers: 52 (Dr. Kari Lounatmaa/SPL), 53 (NASA/SPL), 21 (Dr. Paul A. Zahl); Courtesy of Richard A. Lutz: 9, 11, 46; Superstock, Inc.: 55; U.S. Geological Survey, Denver, CO: 24 (W.R. Normark); Verena Tunnicliffe: 4, 41, 45; Visuals Unlimited: 8 (WHOI/Al Giddings), 23 (WHOI/D. Foster), 13 (WHOI/J.F. Grassle); Woods Hole Oceanographic Institution: 18 (WHOI/Rod Catanach), 7, 51.

Visit Franklin Watts on the Internet at:
http://publishing.grolier.com

Library of Congress Cataloging-in-Publication Data

Gowell, Elizabeth Tayntor
Fountains of life: the story of deep sea vents / Elizabeth Tayntor Gowell
p.   cm. — (A First book)
Includes bibliographical references and index.
Summary: Discusses the formation and discovery of hydrothermal vents and the unusual creatures that can be found near them.
ISBN 0-531-20369-7 (lib. bdg.)   0-531-15908-6 (pbk.)
1. Hydrothermal vents—Juvenile literature. 2. Hydrothermal vent ecology—Juvenile literature. [1. Hydrothermal vents. 2. Hydrothermal vent ecology. 3. Marine animals. 4. Ecology.] I. Title.II. Series.
GB1198.G681998
577.7'9—dc21   97-10924
                                                                                CIP
                                                                                AC

CONTENTS

Scalding hot water billows from a group of rock chimneys called "Smoke" and "Mirrors." Scientists have discovered that amazing animals, like these red-tipped tubeworms, thrive around deep-sea vents.

LIFE AROUND DEEP-SEA CHIMNEYS

Imagine a place where rock "chimneys" as tall as buildings belch black smoky water hot enough to fry an egg. Just a few inches away, giant tubeworms gently sway to and fro, clams as big as footballs wedge themselves among the rocks, and blind crabs scurry about in search of food.

This might sound like the opening of a science fiction novel, but it isn't. Such a place does exist right here on Earth. As a matter of fact, there is more than one such site. They are deep-sea *ecosystems* found along cracks in the seafloor, more than 1 mile (1.6 km) below the ocean's surface.

At the center of each of these remarkable underwater environments is a deep-sea vent—a hot spring—that spouts superheated water full of *sulfide* and other minerals. The seafloor immediately surrounding many deep-sea vents

5.

teems with life. Many of the creatures found here seem too strange to be real.

GIANT TUBEWORMS

Many different types of worms live on land and along the seafloor in shallow regions of the ocean. But none of them are anything like the giant tubeworms that grow in dense clusters around, and even on, the hot rock chimneys. In some places, they are so thick that scientists have reported seeing "forests" of these spineless giants.

Tubeworms are as different from earthworms as they are from arthropods—the group that includes insects, lobsters, crabs, and shrimp. The white tube that protects the tubeworm's soft body is about 1.5 inches (4 cm) in diameter and as flexible as a garden hose. It is firmly anchored to the ocean floor. The bright-red plume at the top of the worm's body can be up to 12 inches (30 cm) long. When a tubeworm senses danger, it pulls its plume down into the safety of the tube. The entire tubeworm, including the red plume and the white tube, may be 8 to 12 feet (2.5 to 3.7 m) tall—taller than the tallest basketball player.

Each plume is made up of about 250,000 tightly bundled tentacles. The tentacles are full of *blood vessels* that collect oxygen and other substances from the surrounding seawater. These materials are picked up by bright-red molecules called

Deep-sea tubeworms extend feathery red plumes to collect oxygen and other substances. These spineless vent dwellers can be taller than you! Some grow to heights of 12 feet (3.7 m).

hemoglobin and carried to other parts of the tubeworm's body. In human blood, hemoglobin transports oxygen from our lungs to other parts of our bodies.

Giant tubeworms are the most common inhabitant of many deep-sea vents. One vent site in the Pacific Ocean was named the Rose Garden after the many giant red-headed worms living there.

MAGNIFICENT CLAMS

Among the tubeworms at the Rose Garden, scientists were surprised to find more deep-sea giants—clams with bright-white shells almost 12 inches (30 cm) long. Each of these clams has a strong, muscular foot. A giant clam wedges its foot into openings between rocks, tubeworms, and other clams to hold itself in place. The clam may also use its foot to move slowly from place to place, though it never travels far from the hot, sulfide-rich water spewed from the vent.

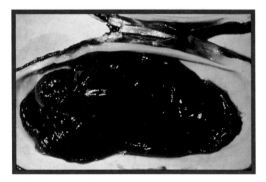

Inside the bright white shells, the flesh of this deep-sea *mollusk* is dark red. One scientist compared it to a piece of steak. But don't add these clams to your dinner menu yet. They are full of sulfide and smell like rotten eggs!

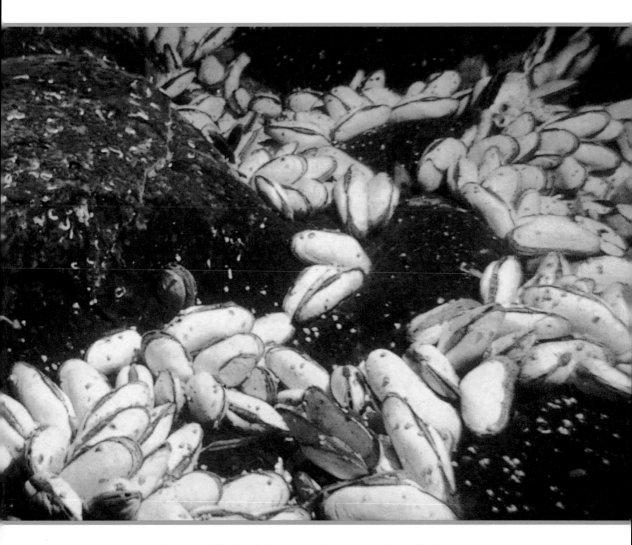

*The dark red flesh of the giant deep-sea clam (facing page)
looks like steak, but smells like rotten eggs. Phew!
Deep-sea clams are as long as footballs. These mollusks
live in dense clusters around many deep-sea vents.*

While some of the best-known deep sea vents have been named for tubeworms, the names of others have been inspired by these magnificent clams. One example is Clambake I. When researchers first saw photographs of this site, they thought it was a deep-sea dump. They assumed that the clam shells they saw scattered on the ocean floor were garbage that had been tossed overboard by a passing ship after a seafood feast. The scientists did not realize how large the shells were, and they never even dreamed that clams could live in the deep sea.

PATCHES OF DANDELIONS

Deep-sea dandelions are pretty, peach-colored creatures about the size of ping-pong balls. These delicate animals look like dandelion flowers that have gone to seed. Their slender tentacles anchor them to rocks on the ocean floor, while their soft, jellylike bodies bob and sway in the gentle currents.

When these fragile jelly animals were first discovered, scientists tried to collect the dandelions so they could study them. But deep-sea dandelions are so delicate that they break apart the moment they are touched. Eventually, scientists designed a special piece of equipment—a clear plastic tube with a quick-release trapdoor—to gather the dandelions.

Scientists were thrilled when they brought the first dandelion up to the surface. Curious researchers in a ship on the surface eagerly awaited the jelly's arrival. But the dainty dan-

*Deep-sea jellies called "dandelions" bob gracefully
among worm tubes at a deep sea vent.*

delion was never intended to be away from its deep-sea home. Within an hour, the gentle jelly fell apart right before the eyes of its admirers.

Scientists have since learned that the deep sea dandelion is a *colonial* creature. In other words, the "flower" is made up of many "petals," and each petal is actually an individual animal. By living and working together, these animals can find food and protect themselves from enemies more easily. The whole creature belongs to a group of jelly animals called *siphonophores*. It is closely related to the Portuguese man-of-war, which is also made up of hundreds of individual animals.

Like other jellies, dandelions have tiny tentacles that radiate out from their central blobby body. These tentacles have *nematocysts*—stinging cells that are the dandelion's hunting and defense system. The chemicals temporarily paralyze enemies as well as *prey*. In some areas, such as the site called Dandelion Patch, scientists have observed hundreds of these peachy puffballs floating just above the ocean floor.

CURIOUS CRUSTACEANS

On nearly every dive to deep-sea vents, researchers find dozens of crabs scuttling among tubeworms and around chimneys. Unlike their crab cousins living in shallow waters along the ocean's edge, vent crabs are as pale as porcelain and unable to see. Some have tiny eyes, but are blind. Others have no eyes

Porcelain white crabs, such as the ones shown in this photo are common inhabitants of deep-sea vent ecosystems.

at all. Because sunlight never reaches the depths of the ocean, eyes are useless there.

Crabs are not the only crustaceans found close to deep-sea vents. Some sites have *galatheids*, which look like miniature lobsters. Many vents in the Atlantic Ocean are home to thousands of thumb-sized rift shrimp that swarm like bees around deep-sea chimneys. These shrimp do not have normal eyes, or even an eyestalk.

In the 1980s, Cindy Lee Van Dover, a researcher and deep-sea submersible pilot now at the University of Alaska, noticed unusual reflective patches on the backs of these shrimp. When she dissected the shrimp, she found that the spots contain a light-sensitive substance found in the eyes of many animals.

Van Dover believed that the spots on the rift shrimp were some type of "eyes," but since the patches have no lenses, they cannot form an image. Van Dover wondered what this creature could see in the darkness of the deep sea. Were the vents giving off a type of light that is invisible to humans? She wanted to find out.

She asked John Delaney, a scientist from the University of Washington, if he would use his electronic digital camera to film the vents. This camera was designed to photograph far-off galaxies in space, so it could detect very low levels of light. The results were exciting—deep-sea vents glow!

Van Dover does not know exactly how seeing the glow helps the shrimp. Maybe they use the light to make sure that

A large cluster of rift shrimp cover the sides of a deep-sea chimney.

they don't move too close to or too far from the vent. If the shrimp get too close to the vent, they might fry. If they are too far away, they may have trouble finding food. This is just one of many questions scientists have about deep-sea vents and the animals that live nearby.

*Oceanographers spend weeks, even months, at a time
on research vessels like the* Knorr *while they study
the mysteries of the deep.*

THE DISCOVERY

It isn't surprising that there's still plenty to learn about deep-sea hot springs. After all, no one even knew they existed until 1977. That's when scientists found the first one—almost by accident.

One evening, a team of scientists was sitting on the deck of the *Knorr*, an ocean research vessel. Miles below the surface, a sled with temperature-recording equipment was being towed along the floor of the deep Pacific Ocean.

When one of the scientists checked the data being sent up from the equipment, she noticed something completely unexpected—a tiny increase in the water temperature. Far from the warmth of the sun's rays, the temperature of the deep ocean should be consistently ice cold. What was heating it up? The researchers didn't have an answer.

Alvin, *a deep-sea submersible operated by Woods Hole Oceanographic Institution, was the first underwater vehicle to explore deep-sea vents.*

To investigate, the oceanographers made a series of dives in a small submersible called *Alvin*. This deep-sea exploration vehicle is operated by the Woods Hole Oceanographic Institution on Cape Cod, Massachusetts.

ALL ABOUT *ALVIN*

Alvin is 25 feet (7.5 m) long—about the length of two station wagons—and can dive to a depth of 2.5 miles (4 km). A pilot and two observers ride inside *Alvin*'s crowded passenger compartment—a metal sphere that is just 7 feet (2 m) in diameter. The outside shell of the sphere is made of *titanium,* one of the strongest metals in the world.

The shell has to be tough because water pressure in the deep ocean is tremendous. Can you imagine the weight of a horse pressing down on every square inch of your body? That's how much weight pushes against objects 2,000 feet (600 m) below the surface. Farther down, the pressure is even greater. The titanium shell of *Alvin*'s passenger compartment protects the crew from being crushed.

Alvin is carried to dive sites all over the world by a "mother" ship. This larger vessel is a floating dormitory, cafeteria, and laboratory for scientists. It is also a service garage and launch pad for *Alvin*. Engineers on board the mother ship inspect *Alvin* carefully before each dive to make sure that all its instruments are working properly. Unlike some deep-sea exploration vehicles, which are lowered into the ocean on cables, *Alvin* is on its own when it is released from the mother ship.

THE JOURNEY TO THE OCEAN FLOOR

From the sunlit ocean surface, *Alvin* sinks slowly—pulled downward by gravity—into the deep sea. After just 15 minutes, *Alvin* is 1,000 feet (300 m) underwater. The passengers inside the vehicle are surrounded by inky blackness. The only light comes from *bioluminescent* creatures swimming nearby.

Many of these animals—fish, shrimp, worms, and squids—have glowing bacteria living on their skin or in special organs inside their bodies. Some of the creatures use their glow to lure prey, while others use it to fool their enemies. One observer described the scene this way: "Flashes of light from luminescent creatures swirled in the darkness past our windows as we descended a mile and a half . . . to the ocean floor."

The trip to the bottom takes about an hour and a half. As *Alvin* approaches the seafloor, the pilot powers up the thrusters, turns on the vehicle's lights, and steers to the research site.

The sabertoothed viperfish uses its backward-facing teeth to trap prey. Few victims escape this deep-sea predator.

THE FIRST DEEP-SEA VENT

The first deep-sea vent was discovered 200 miles (320 km) west of the Galapagos Islands, which are off the coast of South America. More than 1 mile (1.6 km) beneath the ocean's surface, scientists found the warm water they were looking for. They also found something they didn't expect—a seafloor covered with life.

As sensors on the outside of *Alvin* recorded a temperature increase, fountains of hot, shimmering water came into view. Surrounding these spouting hot springs were giant tube-worms, huge clams, and other bizarre creatures. These animals were unlike anything the scientists had ever seen.

The researchers had suspected that underwater hot springs would be the source of the heat, but they never expected to find such a diverse array of animal life nearby. "Isn't the deep ocean supposed to be like a desert?" asked one observer. The crew members couldn't believe their eyes as they stared at the strange scene before them.

Using *Alvin*'s two mechanical arms, the crew collected water, rocks, and clam-shells to show their colleagues on the surface. Meanwhile, scientists on board the mother ship were

Scientists were surprised to find a variety of organisms living around deep-sea vents.

*Prepare to dive! The deep-sea submersible
Alvin is being lowered to the ocean's surface to
begin another expedition to the deep sea.*

jumping around in excitement as they waited to hear more about *Alvin*'s amazing discovery.

Once *Alvin* resurfaced, the scientists got to work. They wanted to examine all the samples brought back from the deep-sea vent. When the jar containing a water sample was opened, scientists quickly ran out of the lab. The water smelled terrible—like rotten eggs!

"We realized that regular seawater was mixing with something," said scientist John Edmond, a *geochemist* from the Massachusetts Institute of Technology (MIT) in Boston. Further tests showed that the water contained sulfide, a toxic form of the chemical sulfur. While this substance is deadly to most living things, it does not seem to bother vent animals. In fact, they need the sulfide to survive.

Since the first deep-sea hot spring was discovered in 1977, *Alvin* has been used to find and study many more vent sites in both the Pacific and the Atlantic oceans. At least 300 new species of animals and bacteria have been identified.

Scientists from all over the world are now studying the vents and the ecosystems that surround them. They have begun to find answers to some very important questions: Why is the vent water so hot? Where does the sulfide come from? How do vent animals survive the heat? Why are the tubeworms and clams so big? And what do these giants eat? With each dive, *Alvin* makes exciting new discoveries and brings back more clues to these secrets of the deep sea.

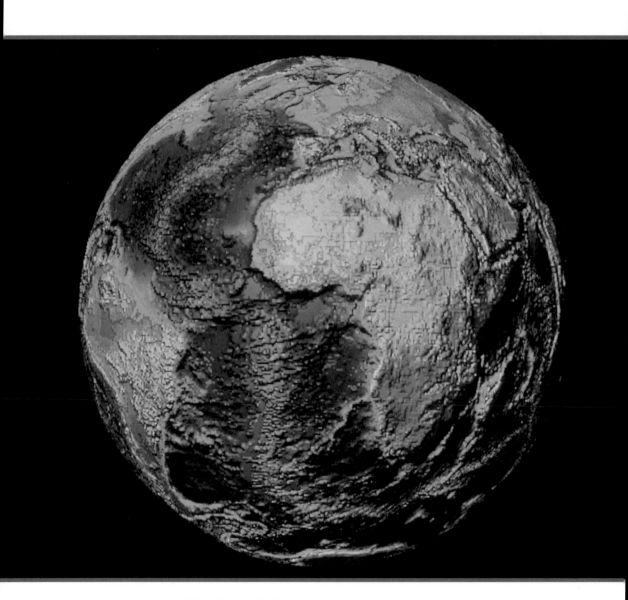

Hidden beneath the ocean's surface, the landscape of the ocean floor includes mountains, valleys, and plains that rival those found on the continents.

PIECES
OF A PUZZLE

Most deep-sea hot springs are found along the *mid-ocean ridge*. This underwater mountain range is more than 40,000 miles (64,000 km) long and winds its way through all the world's oceans. Although most of the mountains in this submarine range are hidden beneath the ocean's surface, the highest peaks rise above sea level to form islands.

One of the largest mountain peaks forms Iceland, a small island in the North Atlantic Ocean. The tallest peak, located in the Azore Islands off the west coast of Africa, rises 27,000 feet (8,000 m) above the seafloor. It is almost as tall as Mount Everest, the highest mountain on land. At the center of the mid-ocean ridge is a giant valley, or *rift*, as big as the Grand Canyon. Along the rift, Earth's outermost layer—the *crust*—is splitting apart and growing through a process called *seafloor spreading*.

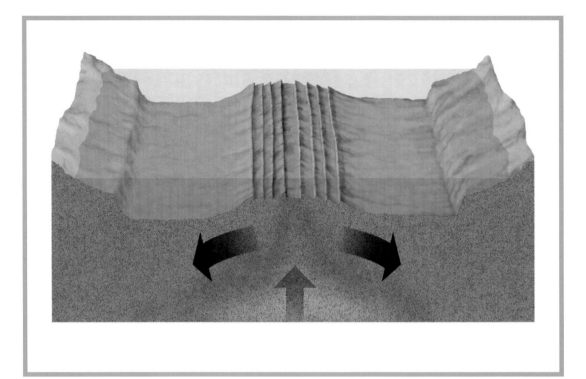

When Earth's plates are pulled apart, magma rises up to the surface, and new seafloor forms.

Earth's crust is made up of seven large pieces, called *plates*, that fit together like pieces of a giant jigsaw puzzle. The plates, which carry the continents and oceans, float on Earth's *mantle*—a layer of soft, molten rock below the crust. Along the mid-ocean ridge, heat from deep within Earth pushes the plates apart, and *magma*, also called lava, moves up to fill the cracks.

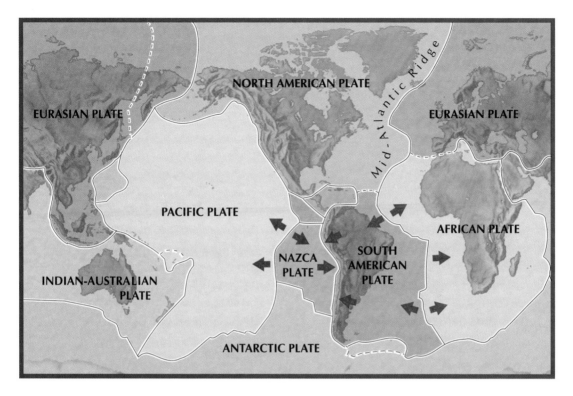

Earth's crust is broken into plates that are constantly moving.
As a result, the continents' positions change over time.

As the magma cools, new seafloor is created. This is what's happening between the Nazca Plate and the Pacific Plate, where the first vent was discovered. It is also happening between the South American Plate and the African Plate, and between the North American Plate and the Eurasian plate.

The total surface area of Earth's crust, however, does not increase. As new crust forms at the ocean ridges, old crust is destroyed at deep-sea trenches. Here, plates are pushed together and one slides under the other. As the lower plate is pushed toward the Earth's center, it melts. This process, called *subduction*, is happening where the Nazca Plate meets the South American Plate.

Earth's plates move very slowly—only 2 to 7 inches (6 to 18 cm) per year. Yet, over time, that movement has been enough to change the face of our planet. Many millions of years ago, all the continents were part of a single landmass called *Pangaea*.

About 200 million years ago, the supercontinent began to split apart. Since that time, the continents have continued to move at a rate of about 12 to 25 miles (19 to 40 km) per million years. This process has slowly created the Atlantic Ocean. Today, the Atlantic is growing larger and larger every year. In another 200 million years, the Earth's surface may look completely different.

About 180 million years ago, Earth had one huge continent—called Pangea—surrounded by a large ocean (A). Over the next 60 million years, Pangea split into two land masses— Laurasia and Gonwanaland (B). As time continued to pass, the land broke into several more pieces. Today, there are seven continents (C).

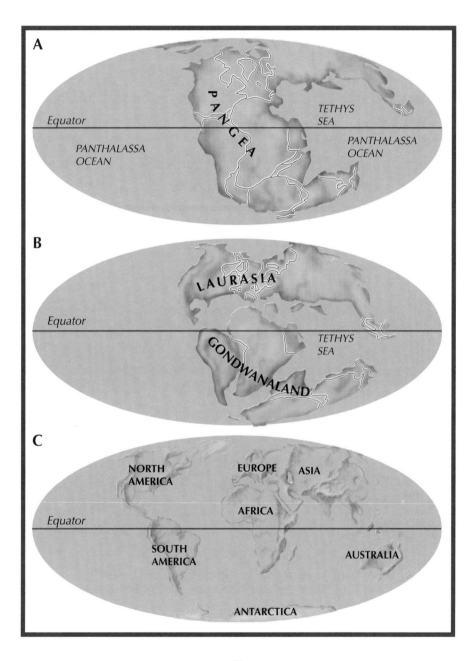

A

Equator

PANGEA

TETHYS SEA

PANTHALASSA OCEAN

PANTHALASSA OCEAN

B

Equator

LAURASIA

GONDWANALAND

TETHYS SEA

C

NORTH AMERICA

EUROPE

ASIA

AFRICA

Equator

SOUTH AMERICA

AUSTRALIA

ANTARCTICA

HOW A DEEP-SEA VENT FORMS

As seafloor spreading pushes Earth's plates apart, ice cold seawater at the bottom of the ocean seeps down through the cracks in the crust. The water may travel more than 1 mile (1.6 km) into Earth's interior until it comes into contact with a zone of very hot rock. This hot rock superheats the seawater, causing it to expand and then rise up toward the ocean floor.

As the hot seawater rises, it dissolves minerals from surrounding rocks and is transformed into a chemical-rich broth. When this hot fluid finally reaches the surface of Earth's crust, it gushes out of the seafloor as fast as water from a fire hydrant. A deep-sea vent is born.

The typical life span of a deep-sea hot spring is probably just a few decades. *Thermal energy* and upwelling magma constantly crack and fill Earth's crust along the mid-ocean ridge, creating and closing the pathways that carry superheated fluids up to vents. How hot is the material that spews from deep-sea hot springs? In the deep ocean, the average water temperature is just a couple of degrees above freezing—34°F (2°C). Scientists were surprised to find that the water close to one of the first known vents was 50°F (10°C). More recently, they have found that the water released by many vents is much hotter—as hot as 700°F (375°C).

Rock chimneys are formed by minerals in vent water. Some tower more than 30 feet (9 m) above the seafloor.

Geysers: Hot Springs on Land

Although scientists have known about hot springs on the ocean floor for only about 20 years, they have been mesmerized by hot springs on land for centuries. These *geysers* seem to form in the same way as deep-sea hot springs. But since air pressure on land is not as great as water pressure in the ocean, the hot, mineral-rich fluid often turns to steam as it explodes from the ground.

There are four major geyser fields on Earth. They

are in Iceland, New Zealand, Russia, and the United States. "Old Faithful," the most famous geyser in the world, is located in Yellowstone National Park in the United States. This geyser erupts every 30 to 90 minutes in an awesome display of water and steam that shoots 165 feet (50 m) into the sky.

ROCK CHIMNEYS: A CLOSER LOOK

As this hot fluid rises in the cold ocean waters, some of the dissolved chemicals form solid particles. These particles often give the water color and make it look smoky. Sulfide compounds color the water gray or black. Other chemicals give it a bluish or milky-white look. Sometimes the chemicals create the shimmering rainbow effect of a large fountain lit up with colored lights.

Deep-sea hot springs that billow clouds of black, sulfide-rich water are called *black smokers*. One submersible pilot reported a black smoker that looked like a "locomotive blasting out black smoke" from a 6-foot (2-m)-tall rock stack. Rock chimneys are built by minerals that form clumps and fall out of the chemical-rich fluid released from deep-sea vents.

The rock chimneys at deep-sea hot springs can form very slowly or very rapidly. *Alvin* once accidentally knocked over a 33-foot (10-m)-high chimney in the Pacific Ocean, just off the coast of Mexico. When scientists visited the same site 3 months later, the chimney had grown 20 feet (6 m)! Time-lapse photographs of another site show that its chimney grew 4 feet (1.2 m) in one day!

Chimneys can reach tremendous heights, some rise more than 30 feet (9 m) above the seafloor. The largest-known black smoker was named Godzilla, after the giant monster in an old science fiction movie. Scientists estimate that Godzilla's chimney is more than fifteen stories high.

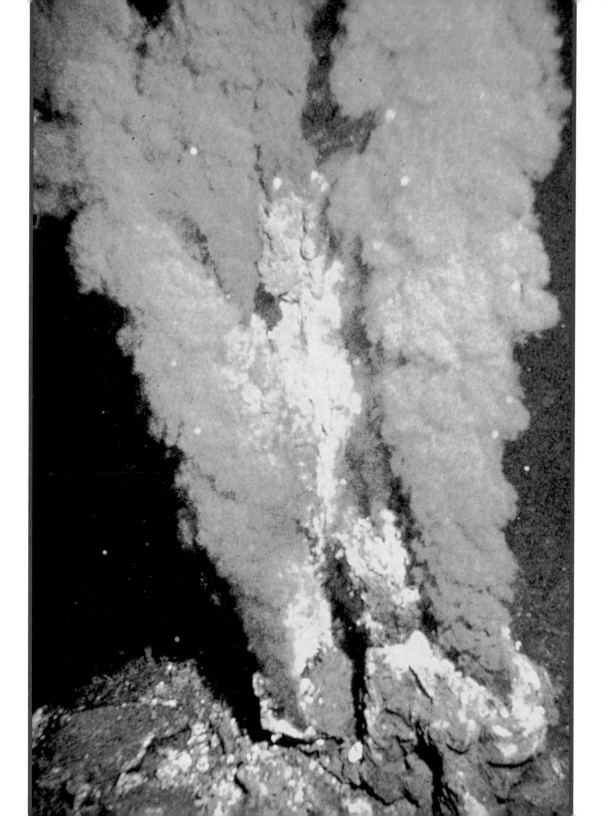

Sometimes the names of deep-sea chimneys are inspired by their unusual shapes. A group of chimneys named Kremlin are covered with formations that look like the onion domes of Russian churches. The Beehive and the Wasp's Nest are rounded mounds with shingle-like surfaces. Other chimneys are named for their discoverers. Two of the chimneys at a site first explored by a team of American and French scientists were named Statue of Liberty and Eiffel Tower. The scientists were so surprised to find this vent site that they named it Lucky Strike!

A fire underwater? No, it's not smoke. These rock chimneys are spouting hot water full of inky sulfides.

chapter

4

DEEP-SEA DINNER

In most environments on Earth, plants and animals get all the energy they need to live and grow from the sun. Plants use energy from the sun's rays to change water and carbon dioxide into simple sugars. This process, called *photosynthesis*, provides the plants with food. When a rabbit, zebra, or small fish eats these plants, some of the energy that came from sunlight is transferred to their bodies. This energy moves farther up the *food chain* when a fox eats a rabbit, when a lion eats a zebra, or when a shark eats a small fish.

In a forest, on an African plain, or in a coral reef, the sun is the ultimate source of food. But sunlight cannot reach the deep sea, so how do creatures survive on the ocean floor? It turns out that plants can't live in the deep sea. Without sunlight to power photosynthesis, plants die.

Most of the animals that live far below the water's surface are scavengers. They eat *marine snow*, tiny bits of waste material that fall from the upper regions of the ocean where the sun supports life. A few animals are *predators*. They eat the animals that eat the marine snow.

Plankton are among the many ocean creatures that feast on marine snow. These leftovers are an important source of energy for most deep-sea animals.

One of the most common deep-sea creatures is the sea cucumber. Like earthworms, these relatives of sea stars eat mud and sand, digesting hidden bits of plant and animal matter that have fallen from above. There are also scavenging crabs, snails, and brittle stars. Worms are common, too. Most lie buried in ooze on the ocean floor with their tentacles extended to catch whatever passes by.

Because marine snow doesn't make a very hardy meal, it cannot support many organisms. As a result, most of the ocean floor looks like a lifeless desert. In this watery wasteland, deep-sea vents are like *oases* teeming with life. Hundreds, even thousands, of creatures live in the area immediately surrounding many deep-sea vents.

SOMETHING NEW ON THE MENU

Why is there so much more life around vents than in other parts of the deep ocean? It's because there is plenty of food. The creatures that live near the vents don't eat scraps of marine snow. Microorganisms manufacture their own food using a process called *chemosynthesis*, rather than photosynthesis. The bacteria and other microbes living on deep-sea chimneys or floating in water closeby use chemical energy supplied by stinky sulfide to convert carbon dioxide into simple sugars. These microorganisms take the place of plants at the bottom of the deep-sea-vent food chain.

Bacteria form thick mats that carpet rocks around many deep-sea vents.

Bacteria for dinner? Crabs and galatheids scavenge for food on bacteria-covered rocks surrounding deep-sea vents.

It may not seem like bacteria would make a satisfying meal. They are so small. Even the "jumbo" bacteria discovered at deep-sea vents are smaller than the head of a pin. But vents spew so much sulfide into the deep ocean that bacteria grow by the trillions, quadrillions, even quintillions. At some vents, floating bacteria form dense clouds that look like an underwater blizzard. At new vents, scientists have observed clouds of bacteria 165 feet (50 m) high and as white as snow. In other places, fuzzy white, green, or yellow mats of bacteria carpet the hot-spring chimneys and surrounding seafloor.

Many animals eat the free-floating bacteria that swirl in the plume of deep-sea vent water. Others graze on the mats of bacteria growing on surrounding rocks. The pink eelpout, a slender fish about 10 inches (25 cm) long, swims head down in the vent water as it feeds on bacteria. Crabs and tiny shrimp-like crustaceans pick microbes from the rocks. When submersible divers collect clumps of bacteria using small vacuum tubes called "slurp guns," they also suck in hundreds of tiny creatures still feasting on their microscopic meal.

While some vent animals munch on mats and clouds of bacteria, scientists have discovered that others have "gardens" of bacteria growing inside them. Biologists have known for a long time that corals have microscopic plants called algae living in their bodies. These algae use waste products from the coral animal along with sunlight to make sugars through photosynthesis. Some of these sugars help feed the coral animal.

Some types of vent bacteria have a similar lifestyle. But they—like their free-floating neighbors—use chemosynthesis, rather than photosynthesis, to make food. This food nourishes the bacteria and their animal hosts. In return, the hosts offer the bacteria protection. When two different types of organisms live and work together like this their close association is called *symbiosis*. A relationship that benefits both organisms, like the coral and the algae, is called *mutualism*.

The discovery of billions of symbiotic bacteria inside the bodies of the giant tubeworms solved one of the great mysteries of deep-sea hot springs. Despite their size, these huge worms have no mouth, no opening to expel wastes, and no digestive tract. It took several years for scientists to figure out how these giants get their food. Tubeworms use their plumes to gather sulfide from seawater. The sulfide is picked up by the red hemoglobin molecules in the tubeworm's blood vessels and carried to the bacteria. It is the hemoglobin that gives a tubeworm's plume its bright-red color.

Many other deep-sea vent animals also have bacteria living in their bodies. The hairy snail is nourished by deep-sea bacteria in two ways. It has chemosynthetic bacteria living in its gills, and it grazes on the mats of bacteria on the chimneys and seafloor.

Giant tubeworms use their bright-red plumes to collect sulfide.

Vent clams are also fed by bacteria living in their bodies. Hemoglobin within the clam's meaty body causes it to look bright-red, just like a tubeworm's plume. The mussels living around deep-sea hot springs also have a symbiotic relationship with chemosynthetic bacteria. They may get additional nourishment from bacteria they trap through *filter feeding*.

These giant clams and mussels live at a vent site called Clambake. Like tubeworms, they have a symbiotic relationship with vent bacteria.

Rift shrimp have symbiotic bacteria growing on the outside of their bodies. Scientists aren't sure why the bacteria are there, but believe they may be very important to the shrimp's nutrition. Rift shrimp use their specially designed front legs to mine metal sulfides from deep-sea chimneys. Apparently the shrimp eat the sulfides to get at bacteria living in and on the rock.

Researchers all over the world were stunned when they learned about the unusual creatures living in deep-sea vent communities. Before this discovery, scientists believed that the sun was the ultimate source of energy for every ecosystem on Earth. "Few discoveries in science come entirely unexpected," says Holger Jannasch, a scientist who works at Woods Hole Oceanographic Institution. "This is one of them."

Today, scientists know that energy from deep within Earth also fuels a number of underground ecosystems. These unusual ecosystems are very important. There is more animal life at some deep-sea vents than there is in an equal-sized area of tropical rain forest. Similarly, the total weight of underground organisms may be equal to that of creatures living on Earth's surface.

Crabs scurry across a rock chimney at the Galapagos Rift in the Pacific Ocean.

chapter

5

FUTURE EXPLORATIONS

Future explorations of deep-sea vents are expected to bring new discoveries and provide answers to some of scientists' questions. These unique ecosystems may also offer clues about other unusual habitats and life forms.

LEARNING MORE ABOUT DEEP-SEA VENTS

The deep sea is the largest habitat on Earth. Nearly 75 percent of our planet's surface is covered by ocean, and 90 percent of the ocean is more than 1,000 feet (300 m) deep. Yet very little is known about the creatures that live in the depths. Few have ever been seen and even fewer have been caught. Collecting deep-sea life from the sea's surface has been compared to collecting rain forest life from a hot-air balloon. Gathering samples with this type of technique can show us only a fraction of all the sizes and varieties of animal life that live far below the ocean's waves.

Thanks to deep-sea submersibles like *Alvin*, we know much more about deep-sea hot springs and their animal communities today than we did 20 years ago, but there is still so much to learn.

Researcher Cindy Lee Van Dover will continue to study the unusual glow of deep-sea vents. She hopes to discover how the light is produced and how vent creatures react to it. Other researchers are trying to understand how vent organisms find new homes when the chimney they rely on stops smoking. Most vent animals have floating or swimming larvae that may travel on ocean currents to new vent sites. How do these larvae find new vents? Do they use some type of chemical clues? Scientists hope to find out.

BETTER MAPS OF THE OCEAN FLOOR

In 1995, using two decades of high-tech satellite data, the U. S. National Oceanographic and Atmospheric Administration (NOAA), created a global map of the ocean floor that contains more information about Earth's deep-sea landscape than any other seafloor map in existence. This new map is so accurate that scientists have said it looks like someone drained the oceans to show the land underneath.

This computer generated view of the Mid-Atlantic Ridge was made from data collected by a research vessel at sea.

With this tool, scientists who study deep-sea hot springs should be able to identify the best locations for future studies. The map will also provide information to help deep-sea oceanographers understand how and why vents form.

TAKING ADVANTAGE OF CHEMOSYNTHESIS

Scientists are investigating the possibility of using chemosynthetic bacteria to "eat" toxic sulfide waste created by mining and some manufacturing activities. These bacteria could be one solution to our toxic-waste-disposal problem.

THE ORIGIN OF LIFE

Some scientists believe that life may have originated in an ancient sea that was warmed by the hot rock that formed primitive Earth. This environment may have had conditions similar to those found at deep-sea vents today. Perhaps the first cells were chemosynthetic bacteria.

Scientists have discovered that some deep-sea-vent microbes belong to a special group of organisms called archaea. Archaea are the most ancient forms of life still alive today. Scientists believe they evolved 3 billion to 4 billion years ago. Studies of these creatures may offer clues about how life began on our planet.

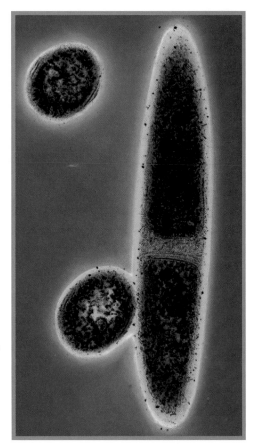

Archaea are among the most ancient creatures still alive today. The long archaea in the middle of this photo is dividing.

LIFE ON OTHER PLANETS

The archaea and bacteria living at deep-sea vents may also offer clues about life on other planets. They thrive in conditions once thought to be too hot and too poisonous to support life. Scientist have begun to wonder if life could be found under similar conditions somewhere else in the solar system.

In 1996, National Aeronautics and Space Administration (NASA) researchers found what appears to be the first evidence of life on another planet—fossils of bacteria. These fossils were found in a meteorite that landed in Antarctica. Scientists believe that this piece of rock came from the surface of Mars. Are these fossils similar to bacteria living around deep-sea vents today?

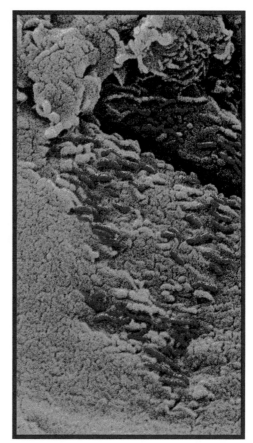

Scientists believe that these tubelike structures are fossils of organisms that lived on Mars more than 3.6 billion years ago. They are colored bright pink in this photograph, so they are easy to see.

If so, life may have traveled here from somewhere else. It might have also traveled to other planets. If the microbes found favorable conditions, they might have survived and prospered.

Some scientists speculate that if liquid water exists below the surface of Mars, life might be present too. There is also evidence that there may be warm seas below the surface of Jupiter's moons. "It's interesting to imagine what we could do 500 years from now, landing on one of these moons, drilling down through the ice, putting a submarine through the ice, and seeing what's there," says one researcher. If there is life beneath the icy layer that covers these moons, does it resemble the creatures that live close to deep-sea vents?

CONSERVATION IN THE DEEP SEA

Scientists exploring the deep sea have been surprised to find so many different types of life. What role do these bottom dwellers play in the ecology of the world's oceans? Have human activities such as ocean dumping disturbed them? What must we do to protect these curious creatures?

In 1994, a group of scientists who study deep-sea vents in the Pacific Ocean created the first deep-sea sanctuary off the coast of Mexico. These researchers agreed to conduct their studies in a way that will preserve deep-sea communities. As submarine technology advances and opportunities for deep-sea exploration increase, similar agreements may be needed in other areas. It is important to protect the strange, yet wonderful, creatures that live at deep-sea vents.

*With each deep-sea dive, scientists learn more
about the vast unexplored territory beneath the
ocean's surface. What other strange and wonderful
ecosystems are waiting to be discovered?*

GLOSSARY

bioluminescent—able to produce light.

black smoker—a deep-sea-vent chimney that spouts a fountain of hot, black, sulfide-rich water.

blood vessel—a flexible tube that transports blood through an animal's body.

chemosynthesis—the process by which microorganisms use the energy of chemical reactions to produce food from carbon dioxide and water.

colonial—pertaining to a group of plants or animals, all of the same kind, that live or grow together.

crust—Earth's outermost layer.

ecosystem—a community of plants and animals and the habitat in which they live, all of which function as a unit.

filter feeding—the process of obtaining food by filtering small particles from relatively large volumes of water.

food chain—a series of organisms that pass food energy from one to another through predation. The smallest organisms in the chain are eaten by the larger organisms, which are then eaten by still larger organisms.

galatheid—a lobsterlike marine invertebrate.

geochemist—a scientist who studies Earth's chemistry.

geyser—a hot spring that occasionally gushes jets of hot water and steam.

hemoglobin—a bright-red blood molecule that carries oxygen.

magma—the molten rock under Earth's crust.

mantle—a layer of molten rock below Earth's crust.

marine snow—the remains of plants and animals that drift down from the sunlit surface waters of the ocean to the depths.

mid-ocean ridge—the undersea mountain range that circles Earth.

mollusk—a soft-bodied invertebrate, usually with a hard outer shell, such as a clam or snail.

mutualism—a form of symbiosis that benefits both organisms.

nematocyst—one of the stinging cells of jellyfish and corals.

oasis—a place protected from surrounding unpleasantness; a refuge.

Pangaea—the supercontinent from which the modern continents were created.

photosynthesis—the process by which plants use the energy of the sun to make food from water and carbon dioxide.

plates—large pieces of Earth's crust.

predators—animals that eat other animals.

prey—animals that are eaten by other animals.

rift—an opening made by splitting.

seafloor spreading—the process of creating new seafloor as Earth's crust is pulled or pushed apart and magma moves up to fill the cracks.

siphonophore—a colonial sea jelly, such as the Portuguese man-of-war.

subduction—destruction, as in the subduction of Earth's crust.

sulfide—a form of the element sulfur that is toxic to most animals.

symbiosis—the close association of two different organisms, in which one or both benefit from the relationship.

thermal energy—energy produced by heat.

titanium—a strong, lightweight metal.

RESOURCES

BOOKS

Cone, Joseph. *Fire Under the Sea*. New York: William Morrow, 1991.

Fodor, R. V. *The Strange World of Deep Sea Vents*. Springfield, NJ: Enslow, 1997.

Van Dover, Cindy Lee. *The Octopus's Garden*. New York: Addison-Wesley, 1996.

MAGAZINES

"Deep Sea Smoke? Not." *Ocean Explorer*, for the Young Associates of Woods Hole Oceanographic Institution, September 1992.

"Hitchhikers on the Larval Highway." *Ocean Explorer*, for the Young Associates of Woods Hole Oceanographic Institution, May 1994.

Monastersky, Richard. "The Light at the Bottom of the Ocean." *Science News Online*. September 7, 1996. http://www.sciencenews.org/sn_arch/

VIDEO

Deep Sea Dive. National Geographic Society, 1993.

INTERNET

Due to the changeable nature of the Internet, sites appear and disappear very quickly. These pages offered useful information on deep-sea vents and ocean exploration at the time of publication.

The Woods Hole Oceanographic Institution (WHOI) home page provides information about WHOI's ongoing oceanographic research and education programs. The marine operations section includes expedition schedules for the *Alvin*. The address is:
http://www.whoi.edu

The Vents Program homepage offers information, photos, and video clips on current deep sea vent research from the U.S. National Oceanographic and Atmospheric Administration's (NOAA's) Pacific Marine Environmental Laboratory (PMEL). It can be reached at:
http://www.pmel.noaa.gov/vents/home.html

INDEX

ABOUT THE AUTHOR

Elizabeth Gowell enjoys exploring the ocean and writing about sea life. She is an award-winning author and environmental consultant. Ms. Gowell has worked for the New England Aquarium; the Massachusetts Coastal Zone Management Program; and SEACAMP, a marine science education program in the Florida Keys. She is a scuba diver and sailor. Ms. Gowell lives in the ocean state of Rhode Island with her husband, Jay, and their children—Emily, Matthew, and Julia.